Mrs. Pinchpenny's Guide to Surviving the Holidays on a Budget

Mrs. Pinchpenny's Guide to Surviving the Holidays on a Budget

by

Mrs. Pinchpenny

Copyright @ 2013 by Mrs. Pinchpenny

MRS. PINCHPENNY'S GUIDE TO SURIVING
THE HOLIDAYS ON A BUDGET

Mrs. Pinchpenny Guide to Surviving the
Holidays on a Budget

Hot Tropica Books Publication
Updated content April 2013

First Published Copyright © March 2009

Copyright © 2013 Mrs. Pinchpenny

Cover illustration copyright © Missy
Lyons

ISBN: None

Published by: **Hot Tropica Books**

Mrs. Pinchpenny's Guide to Surviving the Holidays on a Budget

Blurb:

There is more to life than buying things to fill our home—and more often than not, a full home does not mean a full and happy heart. Mrs. Pinchpenny shares her favorite money saving tips, crafts and recipes for the most popular holidays: Easter, Birthdays, Christmas, Hanukkah, Halloween, and the 4th of July.

These fun but frivolous holidays can slice through your wallet and your budget if you aren't paying attention. Make your holidays memorable and special, with Mrs. Pinchpenny's holiday tips and tricks--not something you remember every time you make a payment on your visa card for the next 6 months.

TABLE OF CONTENTS

HOW TO USE THIS BOOK

In order to make it as easy as possible to reference the money saving ideas, this book has been broken up into easy to use sections on each topic or theme. Mrs. Pinchpenny first shares her opinion about each holiday, and money saving tips for certain areas of that holiday. Then a craft for kids follows that section, and immediately after the craft, a favorite holiday recipe follows.

MRS. PINCHPENNY'S GUIDE TO SURVIVING THE HOLIDAYS ON A BUDGET
© 2013Mrs. Pinchpenny

The holidays whether they are at the beginning or the end of the year, often blow our budget, as we indulge our desires and try to show our love for our friends and family and even value our business relationships with material things.

Do you really think this is going to make us happy and the holiday special enough to remember? Retailers want you to believe it. We spend more money on gifts, decorations, and food than any other time of the year. Retailers make the highest profit from Halloween to Christmas than any other time of the year. Our children are assaulted with commercials making them want the hottest toy or video game especially hard around Thanksgiving. That is one of the reasons I think it is important to address this issue. We don' need a huge number of gifts to make the holidays special.

There could be a variety of reasons you may want to or need to cut back this holiday season. Maybe you are getting tired of paying off credit card bills for the following three months. Perhaps there is a family crisis and you just don't have the money, or it is just time to pa attention to what you are spending. One very good reason is that you can give more to charities if you have more to give. Whatever the reason, I'll be happy to help you with my tips and tricks to surviving the holidays on a budget.

BIRTHDAYS

Who doesn't love birthdays? I think they are
a special way to celebrate the lives of we care
about, but expenses can quickly add if we don't set
a budget and stick to it. I was shocked when I
visited my local bakery and flipped through the
adorable selections of cakes and frosting covered
delicacies. They all looked so yummy, but how
could I choose just one? They had ever cartoon
character my little ones could ever want plastered
on the cake of actual toys they could keep as a
souvenir.

At first I was very impressed. What little
boy wouldn't be happy with a Thomas the Tank
birthday cake? I had to have one, but there was no
price. So I asked. How much is this? Then the baker
behind the counter responded with a huge price tag
of $100.

I must have stood there for a moment with
my jaw hanging open because she gave me this
really fun look. I know cakes are expensive. Sheet
cakes will run $20-40 with nothing on them from
the grocery store, but to get the special fancy kind
the price tag goes up.

At this point, I might have walked away, but
my child was there looking at the cake with me—
helping to choose. How could I let them down? I
didn't want to disappoint my baby, but I did
something I hope was just as fun. I had to tell him I
would think about it but I had an idea for something
I hoped would be just as fun. We went to the toy
department and picked up a little train to put on the
cake.

Then we made a trip down the baking aisle

and he got to pick out the kind of cake and frosting he wanted. I spent $15 including the toy to do a cake myself. Now, I can honestly say it wasn't as cute as the one in the catalog, but I was proud of it and so was my child because they helped to make it.

When I am responsible for organizing a birthday party I try to start with my budget and stick to it. A lot of fun party decorations can be bought at the local dollar store for a dollar each. That leaves the larger items, like cake, food, and the gift to be divided into the total budget.

On our last kids birthday party we made our own invitations and the bug theme was over the top. We used construction paper and made lady bugs with a small white card that said the time and the date. It was fun and we got a lot of neat comments from the parents and the kids.

BIRTHDAY CRAFT
MEMORY BOX

A memory box is someplace you can keep those treasures memories from a special event. You can remember the year, or a birthday, or a special person. Just decorate the box and then fill it with treasures.

List:
Cardboard Box to decorate—tissue box or shoe box
Glue
Paper
Markers

Directions:
1. This is simple and easy to do craft for most children. Choose a small box, such as a shoebox to decorate.
2. Decorate the outside of the box.
3. If you want to decorate the inside of the box, you want to wait for it to dry before doing that.
4. Let the glue dry a day.
5. Fill the memory box with photos, tickets, pressed flowers, rocks, or anything that you want to remember.

BIRTHDAY CAKE RECIPE

I've used several recipes to make my own birthday cake, and even boxed cake mixes, but I liked this one the best. I tend to keep all these ingredients on hand so it's one I don't usually have to go shopping for.

INGREDIENTS:

- 1 cup butter
- 2 cups white sugar
- 1 teaspoon vanilla extract
- 4 eggs
- 3 teaspoons baking powder
- 3 cups all-purpose flour
- 1 cup milk
- 1 pinch of salt

DIRECTIONS:

1. Preheat the oven to 350 degrees F. Grease and flour one 9x13 inch pan or two 8 or 9 inch round layer cake pans.
2. Cream the butter and sugar together until smooth and fluffy. Mix in the vanilla extract.
3. Separate the eggs and set the egg whites aside. Add the egg yolks one at a time to the creamed mixture, beating after each one.
4. Keeping the wet and dry ingredients separate is a key step to keeping this cake light and fluffy. Use a separate bowl for the next step.

5. Measure the baking powder into the flour, sift a little of the flour into the creamed mixture. Continue adding the flour and the milk alternately, while continually beating the mixture. Beat the cake batter until a few air bubbles show.

6. Beat the 4 egg whites with a dash of salt until stiff. Gently fold egg whites into the batter. Pour batter into prepared pan.

7. Bake at 350 degrees F until cake tests done, approximately 25 to 35 minutes.

MRS. PINCHPENNY'S GUIDE TO SURIVING THE HOLIDAYS ON A BUDGET

EASTER

This is a big holiday for the retail stores. According to CNN, consumers spend $13 Billion a year on Easter. It's crazy, right? But if you go into your local retail store during this time, You can see it. They expect people to buy a lot of stuff. The shelf space is growing every year—aisle by aisle and it's taking over the stores seasonal departments. It's the 5th largest holiday we go shopping for. People buy Easter gifts for their kids even if they aren't religious.

The average shopper spends $120 on baskets and gifts. This all really adds up fast and I'm going to share my favorite tips to cut back here at this holiday.

The first thing I do is look for all the free and fun activities we can at community centers and in our city. This year we visited the Easter Bunny and got a free picture from a local photographer. We also participated in a community Easter egg hunt and the kids got to not only see their friends but found quite a few eggs, and toys.

But we still had our own private party and Easter celebration.

One of the fun things people can do is to make a homemade Easter basket. You can take any bucket or basket and have the kids decorate it and color paper to stick on I, but quite honestly we re-use the same basket year after year. It cuts the cost and helps to make me feel better about reusing what we have.

I keep big plastic tubs organized with different holiday decorations and things we re-use. The baskets, the plastic eggs, even the grass is re-used year after year. This keeps my cost to a minimum and my pocketbook happy.

Decorating Eggs is not only fun but it also has become a tradition in our family—and traditions build memories. We spend the day before Easter decorating the eggs and dying them before the Easter bunny comes the next day.

The great thing about plastic eggs is you don't have to worry about them going bad or getting stepped on if they don't get found in an Easter Egg hunt, but if you do it outside, it's not as much of a worry.

I also think the size of the basket doesn't mean anything. If you want to fill the basket full, that's fine, but why not splurge and get one big item instead of twenty smaller items or a ton of candy that the kids will forget about in a week? It's a balance and just a thought.

For my oldest, this year we opted not to buy toys but to buy clothes for her basket. It's not something I wanted to stop doing even if she has outgrown the egg hunts.

Also, if you're going to give candy—just stick to the kind they really love. Don't buy something that will get thrown away.

My last tip for advice is to look around and try to figure out what they may really love. Maybe a picture or a memento that means something. A small item that we give meaning to, may become more important than a stuffed animal we bought at the dollar store.

EASTER CRAFT
MAKING EGG DYE

INGEDIENTS:

- Food coloring
- Vinegar
- Hot Water
- Hard Boiled Eggs

DIRECTIONS

1. In a small bowl or cup, mix ½ cup of hot water, with 1 teaspoon of vinegar, and 20 drops of color. Mix thoroughly.
2. Submerge a hardboiled egg into the water, turning occasionally until the desired color is reached. It should get darker the longer it is in the dye.
3. Remove egg after 2-3 minutes with a spoon and allow to dry on a wire

rack.

EASTER RECIPE
Egg Salad

INGREDIENTS:

- 8 hard boiled eggs
- ½ cup of mayonnaise
- 2 teaspoons of yellow mustard
- ¼ cup chopped green onion
- Salt and pepper to taste
- ¼ teaspoon paprika
- 1 teaspoon of relish (optional)

DIRECTIONS:

1. Peel and chop the hardboiled eggs.
2. Place the chopped eggs in a bowl. Stir in the mayonnaise, mustard, and green onions. If you want to use the relish, stir it in as well.
3. Season with salt and pepper, and the

paprika.

This egg salad is a great way to use the
leftover hard boiled eggs from the Easter Egg Hunt.
Enjoy.

MRS. PINCHPENNY'S GUIDE TO SURIVING THE HOLIDAYS ON A BUDGET

HALLOWEEN

Halloween is fun. We get to dress up and pretend to be someone different than we really are. It's a great holiday and we get to exercise our creativity and our imaginations. Costumes and candy are two of the most expensive items for the holiday.

At this time of year, I like to use coupons for the candy and I try to buy the kind I don't mind eating. If I have to have leftovers I don't want to waste my money. Something else I consider doing is looking at it longer term. If I have leftover M&M packages for instance, I can use those to make cookies for Christmas.

If I really don't want to be bothered, I also look at organizations that may need or want the leftover candy. It's so hard to get the perfect amount and while I don't want to run out, I hate leftovers not getting used. The school system needs candy as rewards for the students and they may appreciate a donation from a parent if you ask.

The costumes can be a little trickier, but we keep a large plastic tub of the costumes we have bought or made and I encourage the kids to go shopping in their own closets once they figure out what they want to be. For instance an old wedding flower girl dress, combined with a tiara from the toy box made up a Prom queen outfit. Pajamas and a few freckles made with eye outliner, and a baby binky and voila---you have a giant baby.

This holiday isn't too bad, it just requires a little thought and preparation.

HALLOWEEN CRAFT
CREATING A CHALKBOARD PUMPKIN

LIST:

- Chalkboard spray paint
- Pumpkin
- Newspaper

DIRECTIONS:

1. This activity should be done outside. Clean off any dirt on the pumpkin. Make a layer of newspaper to set the pumpkin on and catch the overspray.
2. Spray the pumpkin in one layer. Allow to dry before applying a second layer.
3. The pumpkin will have to be flipped and rolled over to coat it completely. Allow to dry between coats and at least 24 hours between writing on it.
4. Write a scary face with chalk and messages to your guests.

HALLOWEEN RECIPE
Caramel Corn

INGREDIENTS:

- 4-5 quarts of popped popcorn, unsalted, unbuttered
- 2 cups firmly packed brown sugar
- 1 cup unsalted butter
- ½ cup dark syrup
- 1 Tbsp Molasses
- 1 teaspoon salt
- ½ teaspoon baking soda

DIRECTIONS:

1. Heat oven to 225 Degrees F. Place popcorn in a large roasting pan and set it aside to later.
2. Use a 2 quart saucepan to combine the brown sugar, butter, dark syrup, molasses and salt.

3. Cook over medium heat, stirring often, until the candy thermometer reaches 250 degrees F or it has reached a hard ball stage. The liquid should be boiling steady for about 12-14 minutes. (If you drop a small amount in ice water it will form a hard ball once it reaches the hard ball stage.)
4. Remove from heat. Stir in the baking soda. The caramel will foam up a little and turn a lighter shade when it is added.
5. Carefully pour the hot mixture over the popcorn in a large roasting pan.
6. Using a wooden spoon, stir the mixture and the popcorn until all the popcorn is coated.
7. Place in oven for 20 minutes. Remove from oven, and stir to coat the popcorn evenly.
8. Return to oven and continue cooking 20 more minutes.
9. Remove from oven and spoon the caramel corn out onto waxed paper. Allow to cool and then break into bite size pieces.
10. Store in a tightly covered container.

4th OF JULY
Independence Day

The 4th of July is a marker of the middle of summer. It's long summer days and a weekend of parties, barbeques, and firecrackers. We have reason to celebrate. We can remember the glory days and why and how we became free as a country or we can just enjoy the gathering of friends and family.

Many restaurant chains offer deals just for this holiday. So it's worth searching the internet and Facebook pages to see what your favorite chains may be offering.

We used to throw big parties every year during this time, and we had fireworks to share with everyone. The food can be expensive but those fireworks are what really costs the big money.

For the last couple of years, my family has stopped doing them altogether. We don't have the worry about the fires, or the cleanup the next day. We go downtown and see the big display of fireworks put on by the city. For us, it's free. It's fun, and they set it to music. This is professional and we could never afford to do anything like this. So it's been great to be a part of it.

4th OF JULY CRAFT
CANDLE HOLDERS

LIST:

- Baby Jars
- Tea candles
- Newspapers
- Waterproof Outdoor paint red/white/blue

DIRECTIONS:

1. Line a table outside to work with newspapers.
2. Paint the empty baby food jars red, white, or blue.
3. Set a tea candle inside of the jar.
4. Wait until night and light it outdoors. Keep a watchful on the burnings candles and never leave a burning candle alone in case of a fire.

4th OF JULY RECIPE
Fried Chicken

INGREDIENTS:
2 pounds of cut up Chicken
2 cups Buttermilk
2 Tbsp Salt
2 Tbsp Paprika
2 teaspoons garlic powder
1 teaspoon cayenne pepper
2 cups Flour
Vegetable shortening to fry

DIRECTIONS:

1. Place chicken in a plastic container
   and cover with buttermilk. Cover,
   and refrigerate for 12-24 hours.
2. Melt about 2 cups of vegetable
   shortening in an iron skillet. It
   should come up about 1/3 of an inch
   in the pan once melted. Keep the oil

at 325 degrees F.

3. Drain chicken in a colander.
    Combine the salt, paprika, garlic
    powder, and cayenne pepper. Season
    the chicken liberally. Dredge the
    chicken in flour and dust off any
    excess.

4.   Place the chicken in the hot oil, skin
    side down. Cook 2-3 pieces at a time
    until golden brown. This should be
    about 10-14 minutes a side. Then flip
    the chicken over and cook the other
    side. The internal temperature should
    reach 180 degrees to be fully cooked.

5. Drain chicken of the grease by
    setting it on a wire rack over a drip
    pan. Serve and enjoy while still
    warm.

HANNUKAH

There is a religious meaning behind this holiday, but like so many others, the retail stores are cultivating a trend of shopping and spending. While this may be a fun part of the holiday, opening presents everyday can get expensive.

I think like anything, we need to remind ourselves and our kids about the real reason behind the holiday. We need to educate our families by reading books, watching movies and teaching them why it is such a special time in the year.

The best thing you can do to protect your wallet is to set a strict budget for each person on your gift giving list and stick to it. If you don't want to spend more than $40 per person, that breaks down to $5 per child per day for the eight days. If you want to give a larger gift one day, then another day spend less. Give the chocolate coins, or the ever wanted dollar bill. Cash is always appreciated by kids.

Shopping all at once or early can help you to not feel as rushed or pressure to buy whatever is left on the shelves.

HANNUKAH CRAFT
STAR OF DAVID METAL CUTOUT

LIST:

- Metal disposable pie plate or tin.
- Permanent Black marker (Sharpie)
- Scissors
- String
- Hammer and nail
- Scrap wood, carboard, or newspaper to protect your table
- Ribbon

DIRECTIONS:

1. Line your worksurface with thick newspapers, cardboard, or use scrap wood.

2. Draw a star of David on the back of the aluminum pie plate.
3. Using sharp scissors, cut out the design safely and dispose of the scraps.
4. At the top of the star use the hammer and nail to make a hole to hang the star from.
5. Insert ribbon and tie a bow to hang it from.

HANNUKAH RECIPE
HANNUKAH POTATO PANCAKES

INGREDIENTS:

- 4 large potatoes
- 1 medium onion
- 2 eggs
- ¾ cup matzah meal
- Salt and black pepper
- Vegetable oil

DIRECTIONS:

1. Grate the potatoes and squeeze to remove the excess water.
2. Chop the onions into very small pieces. Combine with potatoes and mix well in a large bowl.

3. Combine the eggs and mix it well. Add the matzah meal to the mixture. Add a pinch of salt and pepper to your taste.
4. Using a greased hot griddle pan, add about two tablespoons of the mixture per pancake. Flatten the pancakes with a spatula and cook until they are browned on both sides.
5. Place on a paper towel to drain of the excess oil.
6. Serve and enjoy.

MRS. PINCHPENNY'S GUIDE TO SURIVING THE HOLIDAYS ON A BUDGET

THANKSGIVING

The costs involved in this holiday mostly food related, so in order to save money, you will have to make those savings where you shop. You can go to the grocery store and easily come home with a couple hundred dollars worth of food that is meant for one meal. Many restaurants are trying to get in on that action and offering to cater your meal for you. While this saves time, it doesn't save money. That is something we all struggle with how much time we wan to invest versus, how much money we want to spend. With a little planning you can have a great meal, and still not break the budget. This year, I managed to get the entire turkey dinner for my family of four for $30. You can too.

PLANNING THE MEAL

One of the things that my family has done over the last couple of years is split up the work for making this grand occasion. This year we plan to share the responsibility of cooking with our friends and family. We have a potluck with the side dishes. Each guest is assigned a dish to bring and we cook the turkey and some. Those who can't cook can bring something simple like rolls, stuffing, or the cranberry sauce in the can. Because the dishes are assigned, this means a wide selection of food at the dinner table, and no surprises like an entire meal of only stuffing. Those who are traveling a long distance or having hard times of their own, would be excused from having to bring anything.

If you plan to cook the entire dinner yourself, you can still watch your pennies. The trick is to go shopping with a list of what you need and stick to it. Look over the papers that are having sales the weeks before. You'll notice they all have the traditional items you will need for your

MRS. PINCHPENNY'S GUIDE TO SURIVING THE HOLIDAYS ON A BUDGET

Thanksgiving day meal on sale because they want your business. You should shop at the stores that offer the best sales on the things you need. Now is not the time to be loyal, you need to be loyal to your pocketbook not the store.

If you look closely in the sales flyers you will find that some of the stores even offer turkeys for fee or at a reduced price with a minimum purchase. That is how we managed to get our entire dinner for only $30.

Timesaving tip: When cooking your turkey, use a turkey bag to cook it in the oven. This will save you time in basting the turkey and brown it perfectly.

DECORATING YOUR TABLE

Decorating your table doesn't have to be extravagant or fancy. Some of my most memorable moments include family working together on simple craft projects. Have children help to set the table and make placemats, and napkin rings. You can use Fall colored decorations that you already have, and nature provides some of the most beautiful decorations for free. Have fun with it. Use brightly colored fall leaves to scatter on a tablecloth. Make a centerpiece with a bowl of pinecones, or a leftover pumpkin from Halloween. Remember this holiday is about giving thanks and spending time with your family not gold studded centerpieces or a picture perfect dinner table straight out of a Martha Stewart magazine.

Giving thanks is what Thanksgiving is supposed to be about. Most of the time, we forget, stuffing our faces and bellies full until nearly bursting.

My family has tired different things over the years to show our thanks. It teaches our kids about compassion and appreciation of our lives and our love for one another. One year, we spent the day serving other families in need at a local nursing home. Some people will feed the homeless at the local shelter. How you spend your Thanksgiving is up to you, but I hope you spend it building memories to last a lifetime.

THANKSGIVING CRAFT
TURKEY HANDPRINT

LIST:

- Paper
- Markers

DIRECTIONS:

1. This simple craft is very entertaining to young children. Simple trace their hands on the paper and then close the circle where the wrist is.
2. Color in the fingers as feathers, add a little face and feet and voila! You now have a turkey hand.

THANKSGIVING RECIPE
CLASSIC BREAD AND CELERY
STUFFING

INGREDIENTS:

- 1 loaf of white bread (1 pound)
- ¾ cup of butter
- 1 onion chopped
- 4 stalks of celery
- 2 teaspoons of poultry seasoning
- Salt and pepper to taste
- 1 cup chicken broth

DIRECTIONS:

1. Let bread slices air dry for 1-2 hours and then cut into cubes.
2. In Dutch oven, melt butter or margarine over medium heat. Cook onion and celery until soft. Season with poultry seasoning, salt and pepper. Stir in bread cubes until it is evenly coated. Moisten with chicken broth and mix well.
3. Chill for 30 minutes. Cook in buttered dish for 30-40 minutes at 350 degrees F.

CHRISTMAS

Everything at Christmas seems to sponge up our resources and money. Where do I start? Gifts, cards, decorations, food, it all has a high cost. How do you manage to share your love for everyone and still stay on a budget? Planning in advance.

Cards are one of the easier things to save on. Why do we spend so much time sending out a Christmas card each year, drawling our signature across each one of the cards, and spending nearly a half dollar to send out each one? We could just as easily send out an e-card for free and save ourselves quite a bit of money and quite possibly time if you make a simple hello letter to each one.

Gift buying should be thought of in advance. The last minute shopper is a desperate shopper and does not get the best deal. You should make a list of people that you expect to buy for and set a dollar limit for each one.

Make this a handmade Christmas. Not only can this help to build special memories, but the person receiving the gift knows you gave a part of your heart when you made it. Children can be involved by making jewelry, artwork, and photo frames with their picture in it. Grandparents will especially love this.

Gift Exchanges may happen at work, but have you ever thought about having one for your family? This can help everyone not spend quite as much. You can set a dollar limit, make it a theme exchange. Why not have a year where everyone exchanges a new ornament for the tree? This can be fun in so many ways, and the stealing gifts back can be downright comical.

Our electric bill is often something we forget until it gets here, but with the lights and outdoor decorations it can double or triple a normal electric bill. So what can you do to help cut this? Timers are great. It makes sure that the lights are on after dark when people can enjoy them and are turned off when everyone has gone to bed.

    In decorating your house, be creative. Some
of the best decorations can't be bought. Remember
your own childhood, and how much fun it was to
decorate the tree using a string of popcorn? This is
how you make memories for your children. Make
play dough tree ornaments and then cook them in
your oven, and paint them afterwards. It's simple,
and recipes can be found online.

    One of my favorite things to do is to go
hiking in the Fall and pick up pinecones. These can
be spray painted or used natural, or even dip the
edges in glue and glitter for a glamorous effect.
Then you can use them throughout the house in
your decorating and as centerpieces or on the
fireplace mantle. It's a fun family activity and it
adds to the Christmas spirit. I have even used
smaller pinecones in wreaths and on packages with
a small red bow. It's a simple thing that takes very
little time and money, but the best things about the
holidays can't be bought.

    And memories can't be bought either. They
are made.

    Have you ever thought of buying a fake

MRS. PINCHPENNY'S GUIDE TO SURIVING THE HOLIDAYS ON A BUDGET

Christmas tree? This could easily save your family a $100 or more. Over time, they can save your family money. Not only are they economical, but they are environmentally safe. Consider saving a real tree this year and buy a fake one.

Storing the Christmas items can save you money. After Christmas is when everything to do with the holiday is 50% off. Except for food and candy gifts, but they don't hold up in storage anyway. A small investment now will mean double the savings next year when everything is full price again.

Hopefully, all these ideas will help you all to have a Christmas that you won't be remembering every time you pay your Visa bill. We don't have to buy things we can't afford to impress other people that half the time we don't even like. Change starts with the small things.

Stay cheap!
Mrs. Pinchpenny

CHRISTMAS CRAFT
MAKE YOUR OWN X-MAS CARDS

LIST:

- PAPER
- Pens
- Markers
- Glue
- Glitter

DIRECTIONS:
1. Fold paper in half in the middle.
2. On the front cover, decorate the flap with a cute Christmas greeting.
3. On the inside write the greeting and a personal letter for an extra special touch.

CHRISTMAS RECIPE
SUGAR COOKIES

INGREDIENTS:

- 2 ¾ cup all purpose flour
- 1 teaspoon baking soda
- 1 cup butter softened
- 1 ½ cup white sugar
- 1 egg
- 1 teaspoon vanilla extract

DIRECTIONS:

1. Preheat oven to 375 Degrees F.
2. In a small bowl combine the flour, baking soda, and baking powder, set aside.
3. In a large bowl, cream together butter and sugar until smooth. Add vanilla and eggs and mix thoroughly.
4. Gradually blend in dry ingredients. Roll rounded spoonfuls onto an ungreased cookie sheet.
5. Bake 8-10 minutes in the pre-heated oven or until golden brown. Let stand for one to two minutes and then use a spatula to remove onto wire racks to cool.

www.ingramcontent.com/pod-product-compliance
Lightning Source LLC
Chambersburg PA
CBHW020949180526
45163CB00006B/2376